Let's Say Hello!

Written by Jillian Powell
Illustrated by Stefania Colnaghi

WAYLAND

Rosie went for a jeep ride.

The jeep went into
the park.

"Look Rosie!" Dad said.
"There's a giraffe!"

Rosie wanted to say hello to the giraffe, but it was too busy eating leaves.

Rosie saw some elephants.

"Can we say hello to the elephants?" she asked.

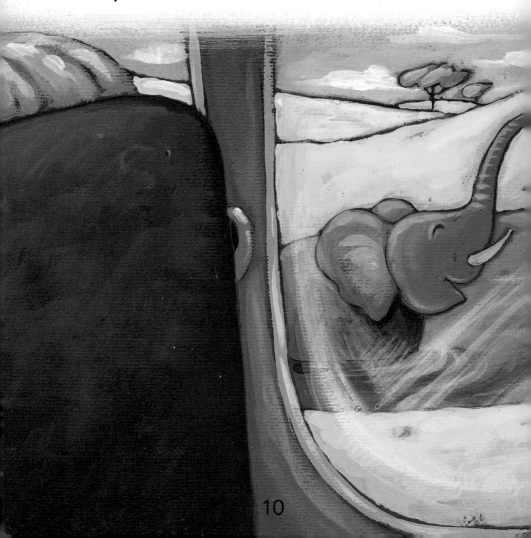

But they were too busy
having a bath.

Next she saw a hippo.
"Hello, hippo!" Rosie said.

But the hippo didn't
see Rosie.

It was too busy swimming.

"Let's say hello to the lions," Rosie said.

"Hello, lions!"

But the lions were too
busy sleeping.

"The monkeys are not
sleeping!" Rosie said.

But the monkeys didn't say hello.

They were too busy playing.

Then Rosie saw an ice cream van.

"Can I have an ice cream please, Dad?" she said.

Dad stopped to get
ice creams.

The monkeys stopped
playing and came over to
the jeep.

They had seen Rosie's
ice cream!

"Now the monkeys want to say hello," Rosie said.

"They like ice cream too!"

START READING is a series of highly enjoyable books for beginner readers. They have been carefully graded to match the Book Bands widely used in schools. This enables readers to be sure they choose books that match their own reading ability.

The Bands are:

Pink / Band 1
Red / Band 2
Yellow / Band 3
Blue / Band 4
Green / Band 5
Orange / Band 6
Turquoise / Band 7
Purple / Band 8
Gold / Band 9

START READING books can be read independently or shared with an adult. They promote the enjoyment of reading through satisfying stories supported by fun illustrations.

Jillian Powell started writing stories when she was four years old. She has written many books for children, including stories about cats, dogs, scarecrows and ghosts.

Stefania Colnaghi lives with her husband in a small village near Pavia, in northern Italy. She loves drawing animals and naughty children and, in her free time, enjoys walking in the hills around her home with her dogs.